MANAGERIAL PROMOTION: THE DYNAMICS FOR MEN AND WOMEN

MANAGERIAL PROMOTION: THE DYNAMICS FOR MEN AND WOMEN

Marian N. Ruderman
Patricia J. Ohlott
Kathy E. Kram

Center for Creative Leadership
Greensboro, North Carolina

The Center for Creative Leadership is an international, nonprofit educational institution founded in 1970 to advance the understanding, practice, and development of leadership for the benefit of society worldwide. As a part of this mission, it publishes books and reports that aim to contribute to a general process of inquiry and understanding in which ideas related to leadership are raised, exchanged, and evaluated. The ideas presented in its publications are those of the author or authors.

The Center thanks you for supporting its work through the purchase of this volume. If you have comments, suggestions, or questions about any CCL Press publication, please contact the Director of Publications at the address given below.

Center for Creative Leadership
One Leadership Place
Greensboro, North Carolina 27410
336-288-7210 • www.ccl.org

Center for
Creative
Leadership®

CCL No. 00224

Library of Congress Cataloging-in-Publication Data

Ruderman, Marian N.
    Managerial promotion : the dynamics for men and women / Marian N. Ruderman, Patricia J. Ohlott, Kathy E. Kram.
      p. cm.
    Includes bibliographical references.
    ISBN 978-1-60491-860-1
    1. Women workers—Promotions—United States—Decision making. 2. Diversity in the workplace—United States. I. Ohlott, Patricia J. II. Kram, Kathy E., 1950- .
III. Title.
HF5549.5.P7R828 1996
658.3'126—dc20   95-52022
                                                        CIP

Table of Contents

Preface vii

Introduction 1

Method 3

    The Company 3

    Sample and Methodology 3

Findings and Analysis 4

Discussion 11

    Decision-making Processes 11

    The Formal Push Toward Diversity 14

    Consequences for Individual Development 15

Implications: Enhancing the Promotion Decision Process 16

    Assessment of Current Practices 17

    Modifications in Human Resources Systems and Practices 18

    Provision of Personal Opportunities for Learning 20

Conclusion 22

References 23

Appendix 27

Preface

This report is an expanded version of the article, "Promotion Decisions as a Diversity Practice," published in 1995 as part of a special issue of the *Journal of Management Development* on gender issues in management development (volume 14, issue 2, pp. 6-23). The journal, published by MCB University Press in West Yorkshire, England, serves as an international communication medium for all those working in the management development field. We decided to publish this version of the journal article so that more of our primary audience of American managers, academicians, and human resources practitioners would have access to the information.

This report differs from the article in the *Journal of Management Development* in some respects: A table has been added, which gives detailed descriptions of the categories of findings, and the interview questions used in the study are reproduced in the Appendix.

Introduction

Although women and nonwhite males have made considerable progress in ascending to management ranks in the last twenty years, it is generally acknowledged that the rate of their advancement has not kept pace with their increasing educational achievements and career commitments (Catalyst, 1990; Sharpe, 1994). Many organizations are taking aggressive steps to rectify this situation by instituting special practices and programs to improve management diversity. Some of the most effective strategies for facilitating the advancement of women and people of color into senior management include: training; a broad range of experiences, including line responsibilities; senior management support; deliberate development and tracking of women and people of color; attitudinal changes on the part of supervisors and senior managers; and mentoring (Catalyst, 1990; Morrison, 1992).

One organizational practice affecting women's mobility which has received little research attention is the process by which promotion decisions are made (Ferris, Buckley, & Allen, 1992). This report proposes that the promotion decision process contributes to the differential advancement of women and men in organizations. In support of this proposition, the actual promotions of thirteen women and sixteen men at a company known for its diversity practices were compared.

Promotions to jobs that provide challenges and develop critical managerial skills and perspectives are important to a manager's future career success (McCall, Lombardo, & Morrison, 1988). For example, different experiences for women and men in the United States Navy have been found to result in different performance evaluations and recommendations (Thomas, 1989). Women may also be given promotions to create the appearance of increased opportunity and responsibility (Flanders & Anderson, 1973), when in reality they are promoted to positions that are not as vital to their organizations as those of men (Powell & Maniero, 1992). Discrimination against women managerial applicants may be most severe when the job requirements are challenging and demanding (Rosen & Jerdee, 1974).

The research literature discusses a number of forces that affect the promotion process (Perry, Davis-Blake, & Kulik, 1994). First, organizational practices for assigning jobs may limit opportunities for women. Women are

Reprinted, with changes, from the *Journal of Management Development,* guest editors Kimberly S. McDonald and Linda M. Hite (Bradford, West Yorkshire, United Kingdom: MCB University Press, 1995) by permission of the publisher. ©1995, MCB University Press.

assigned to less critical positions and divisions than men (Kanter, 1977) and tend to be clustered in staff roles, such as public relations, or in areas where they serve as technical specialists or experts rather than having decision-making responsibilities. Such practices limit mobility for women because early career positions are critical for future advancement in management (Rosenbaum, 1979).

Second, cultural images of men and women affect their working relationships. Most large organizations were created many years ago and have been managed since by a rather homogeneous group of people. Norms, values, rules, and policies established and perpetuated by the dominant group reflect its own values and cultural biases, which may be in conflict with the culture and values of today's more diverse organization membership. (For an in-depth analysis of the structural, cultural, and social-psychological forces shaping differential treatment of nontraditional groups and innovative intervention strategies, see Cox, 1993.)

Third, cognitive biases of individual decision-makers influence the process (Ruderman & Ohlott, 1990). Most people prefer to interact with others they readily identify with and perceive to be similar to themselves (Kanter, 1977) because it may be easier to establish rapport and predict behavior. Individuals who are different are often stereotyped or ascribed characteristics on the basis of their group membership.

The forces mentioned above help us understand the experience of women and members of other nondominant groups in organizations, and they play important roles in affecting women's advancement opportunities. However, we believe that each explanation alone can't completely account for the slow progress of women to upper-management levels. A combination of these forces is likely to shape the promotion process, and thus a more thorough investigation of promotion decisions is necessary. We believe that problems in the way job assignments are made contribute to the differential advancement of women and men.

In this report we examine gender differences in a study of actual promotion decisions made in one American Fortune 500 company and discuss possible explanations for and implications of the findings. We suggest that once these gender differences in promotions are understood, a more appropriate distribution of assignments can be developed, and we offer strategies to accomplish this based on the results of our study and our experiences in several organizations.

Method

In 1989 and 1990 the Center for Creative Leadership conducted a study of the dynamics of promotion decisions in three American Fortune 500 manufacturing companies (Ruderman & Ohlott, 1994). One of the companies asked for an analysis of the differences in promotion dynamics for men and women managers. This particular company had invested considerable resources in a diversity initiative and wanted to understand the impact of the initiative on the promotion decision process. We were also interested in promotion as a diversity practice and saw this as an opportunity to look at similarities and differences in the characteristics of promotions for men and women.

The Company

The management practices of the company have been cited for their exceptional quality in numerous business publications. The company engages in many of the diversity practices discussed in Morrison's (1992) study of organizations recognized for model diversity programs and has often been cited by the press for its commitment to diversity. It has a CEO committed to developing diversity throughout the organization, gender and racial-awareness programs, supervisor-training programs, deliberate development and tracking of white women and men and women of color, mentoring programs, and company-sponsored associations for women and people of color.

Sample and Methodology

We studied the promotions of 13 white women (average age was 37) and 16 white men (average age was 38) to middle and upper management. Men averaged 12 years with the company, and women averaged 8.5 years. *Promotion* was defined as a change in job level along with a commensurate increase in responsibility and pay.

The promotions, all identified by a senior human-resources executive, took place between 1987 and 1989. The interviews were conducted within two years of the promotion in question. Almost all of the women promoted to these levels of management during this time are in the sample. The men came from divisions and functions similar to the women and received promotions that the senior human-resources representative considered to be typical.

For each promotion decision, we interviewed the person promoted, the promoting boss, the promoting boss's boss, and a knowledgeable human-resources representative. All but one of the promoting bosses and their bosses were white males. The interviews were semistructured and covered the events leading up to the promotion, the candidate's career history, and his or her on-the-job relationships (see Appendix). We also reviewed relevant succession-planning documents. From the differing perspectives we developed a summary of the events leading up to each promotion. We then looked across the summaries from this company (as well as those from the two other companies in the original study) for similarities and differences. Through this examination we developed a categorization scheme consisting of thirty-six reasons for promotion which are grouped into five broad categories: preparation, attitudes, people skills, personal attributes, and context (see Table 1). Each promotion case was coded to see how many of the thirty-six reasons applied. A reason was considered relevant to a particular case if mentioned by any one of the following: the promoting boss, the boss of the promoting boss, and the human resources representative. Each case was characterized by multiple reasons. Two researchers jointly coded the data. There was 88% interrater agreement between the codings of the two researchers and a third independent coder.

Findings and Analysis

We used chi-square tests to see if reasons given for promotion differed for women and men. In cases where chi-squares were inappropriate, a Fisher's exact 2 x 2 test was used. Because this was an exploratory study with a small sample, we considered differences between men and women significant if there was less than 10% probability the differences occurred by chance (Hays, 1973).

We found more commonalities than differences between women and men. All promotions were based on the combination of proven competencies and the potential for development. For both groups, credentials, experience, track record, skills, work ethic, ability to work on a team, interpersonal skills, and the potential for growth were frequently mentioned reasons.

There were, however, some differential trends in the accounts of promotions of men and women (see Figure 1). These differences involve some of the more subjective features of the promotion process and are consistent with some of the forces outlined earlier in this paper.

Table 1
Reasons for Promotion of Men and Women Candidates

PREPARATION

Track Record of Success: Has a track record of succeeding in projects, indicating he or she has been tested and proven.

Change Agent: Has successfully implemented a change in the past, thereby improving a situation. The change may be in any arena: technological, administrative, quality, interpersonal, managerial, commercial, or manufacturing. He or she is results-oriented and proactive.

Right Combination of Credentials: Has the right blend of experiences, training, and competencies for the job.

Broad Knowledge of the Organization: Experience in the organization has varied and provides a basis for understanding events outside the home division. Understands the culture, what makes the company tick. Knows where bodies are buried; who knows what.

Experience Adds Utility to Group: Brought an experience that added to the collective expertise of the group.

Technical Skills: Has outstanding expertise in a functional area.

Readiness: Has put in the appropriate amount of time. Has paid his or her dues. Has received recognition for work already done.

ATTITUDES

Work Ethic: Has demonstrated commitment to the company, department, or product with lots of initiative and a can-do attitude. Has shown an eagerness to get things done and is dedicated.

Good Citizen of the Organization: Has made contributions outside the scope of his or her job, such as recruiting a diverse work group, acting as a mentor, or championing a company-wide initiative.

PEOPLE SKILLS

Interpersonal Skills: Has strong interpersonal and communication skills which were noted in a general way.

Team Player: Has acceptance by other members of the staff and adds value to the team.

Table 1 (continued)

Team Builder/Leadership: Able to demonstrate the ability to get people to commit and to work together as part of a team without kicking them in the process. Able to coach and develop people. Can mobilize and marshal people to achieve a goal.

Influence Skills: Has credibility with other units, customers, partners, or industry representatives and can effectively interface with them.

Comfort Level with Superiors/Known Quantity: Was a known entity and could successfully interface with the boss or his or her superiors. The boss was comfortable with and had trust in the candidate. Is credible to upper levels of management.

Emotional Competence: Demonstrates a genuine sensitivity and caring for others.

PERSONAL ATTRIBUTES

Intelligence: Exercises good judgment, articulate, bright, able to extract the essence of complex situations. Is quick on one's feet.

Analytical Abilities: Is rational and practical when making decisions.

Potential for Growth: Demonstrates capacity for growth and is considered a possibility for further advancement in the system. Is able to pick up new knowledge.

Creative: Has innovative problem-solving abilities. Is a novel thinker who sees new directions and possibilities.

Personal Strength/Character: Is willing to take risks, demonstrates maturity, accepts responsibility, and is able to handle tough business decisions. Is able to challenge superiors when necessary. Has self-confidence in uncharted waters, and speaks own mind.

Style: Has presence, stature, and shows sizzle in presentations. Projects an image of a leader. Is smooth and a good socializer.

Business Smarts: Has a strong sense of the business and how to identify and solve business problems. Has a sixth sense for making deals. Is able to read customers' requirements and turn them into plans.

Accountable and Responsible: Follows through relentlessly. Understands responsibilities. Has high integrity.

Able to Work the System: Can bring resources together. Can make large organizations respond.

Strategic Thinker: Is able to think broadly beyond one's own area to the bigger picture; engages in long-range planning.

Table 1 (continued)

CONTEXT

Right Place/Right Time: Happened to have the necessary mix of skills and qualifications at just the time when the job became available.

Groomed for Job: Was supported by someone higher in the hierarchy and was prepared for the job or one like it. In some cases someone higher than the boss pushed for him or her to be offered the job.

Developmental: The job was seen as a growth opportunity which would develop specific skills or prepare the person for a specific job. In some cases the job was seen as a growth opportunity because the boss was good at developing people. In some cases the job was a test or proving ground.

Available: Was freed up from previous job responsibilities usually because of some type of reorganization.

Indispensable to Function: Was essential to the business or project because he or she had substantial background and history that could not be duplicated.

Pushed for Job: Played a major role in convincing the boss or company that he or she deserved a promotion.

Equity: Was promoted for purposes of fairness. May have been led to believe that he or she would be promoted into that job or may have complained to the boss that previous incumbents had been at a higher level. In some cases the promotion was to recognize an increased level of responsibilities or to ameliorate the awkwardness of not having received another job.

Retention: Was promoted in order to keep his or her talents in the company or division. Without the promotion he or she might have left.

Diversity: Adds to the number of high-level white women or people of color in leadership roles, supporting the organization's policies.

Vacancy Demanded Attention: The job had been vacant so long or was vacant at such a crucial time that the pressures to fill it were overwhelming.

Continuity in Location, Function, or Business: Was an insider who knows the culture, technology, and values of the organization.

_____One of the key differences relates to personal judgments of confidence in the candidates. Executives making a staffing decision basically look for someone they have confidence will succeed. This sense of confidence was described differently for men and women candidates. When decision-makers spoke about promotions of men, they often (75% of the cases) mentioned a high level of comfort with the candidate. This meant they knew the candidate and had successfully interacted with him before. For example, one boss said, "I feel very comfortable with him. I know his strengths and weaknesses. I know how he's going to behave. Our relationship is an effective one. I know I can count on it being stable and consistent throughout time." Additionally, bosses reported that prior to the promotion, their superiors or top management found the candidate credible. Comfort level was mentioned less often for women (23% of the cases). Instead, confidence in women candidates was described in terms of their personal strength (31% of the cases). Bosses said that these women had demonstrated a willingness to take risks, to challenge superiors when necessary, and to accept responsibility. For example, one woman was described as a risk-taker with "fire in her belly," willing to challenge past practices and ideas. Such strength of character was never offered as a rationale for men; only women were described this way.

Another key difference relates to the degree to which the new job was unfamiliar to the person promoted. We noticed that some of the women in the

Figure 1
Differential Trends Between Men and Women in Reasons for Promotions

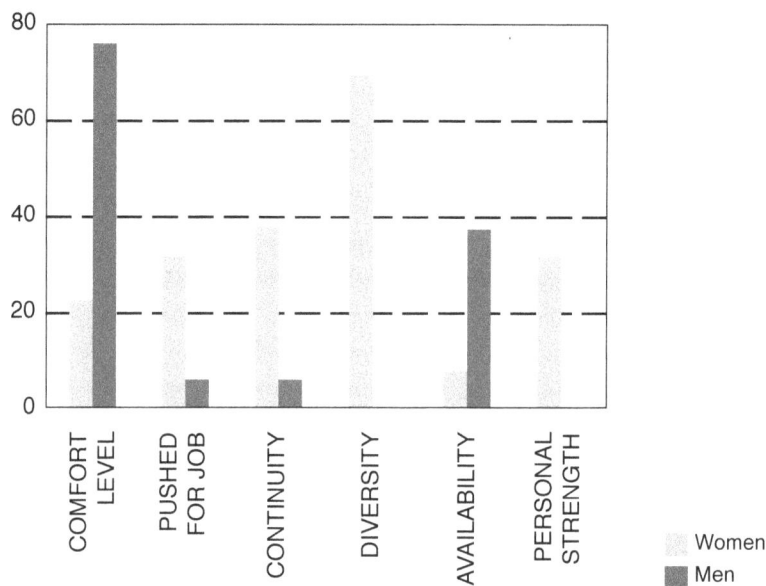

study had been working for the promoting boss before they got the promotion. When they originally started working for that boss, they were put in at a level below the one customary for that job and were told that if they did extremely well they would get a promotion. The first job was described as some kind of apprentice or trial period. Women tended to have to lobby to get the second job by convincing the boss they were ready for promotion. This situation was reflected in the reason for promotion called *pushed for job*—31% of the women were described as having done this. Only 6% of the men were described this way. Women were frustrated by this experience, which was not always appreciated by their bosses. One boss said:

> She is very ambitious, and I thought that being offered this job, the creative playground it offered and the $3 million in resources would be enough for her. But when I brought her in at a level 59, she really wanted to know when she would become a level 60. I told her when the time was right, I'd promote her. I said "soon," and "soon" is under one year. The next day I came into my office, and there was a big card on which there was a blown-up definition of "soon" from Webster's. She got the level 60 soon after that.

The manager and her hiring boss had different impressions of this situation. He saw it as a chance to give her an opportunity to use her skills while she developed them. She was frustrated by the trial period and experienced it as a lack of faith. She pushed for the higher level job because she felt she deserved it.

The tendency to promote women to jobs with highly familiar responsibilities is evidenced in the degree to which continuity was mentioned as a reason for promotion for men and women. *Continuity* means that the person promoted already had intimate knowledge of part of the new job. Examples include moving from head of a key manufacturing department to plant manufacturing engineer or moving from product manager to senior product manager. Continuity was mentioned by 38% of the women and 6% of the men. Thus, bosses are more likely to move women to jobs strongly connected to previous experiences. One woman's boss explained that although the woman had been well prepared for a higher level job for a period of time, he kept her in the same job until a slot opened up in her plant because he thought it would be easier for her to handle new responsibilities if the people were the same. He thought this was important because he believed women have to work harder than men to establish credibility with their co-workers, and it would be easier for her to succeed in a new job in a location where she already had credibility. Although she liked the plant, the woman in this situation found it restrictive to wait for the right opportunity to open up and would have preferred to have taken a similar opportunity sooner, elsewhere. For men, continuity was mentioned less often, and the degree of unfamiliarity between two jobs was greater.

Corporate personnel objectives played different roles in the promotions of men and women. For 69% of the women, the strong corporate emphasis on diversity was mentioned. Decision-makers explained that not only was the candidate well qualified, but the promotion had the extra benefit of adding to the number of women in upper-level positions. For example, one boss said, "She was the best overall for the corporation . . . technical background, MBA, credentials, line experience. In addition, we were looking to move women up the corporate hierarchy, and she looked like a good fit." Obviously, diversity was not mentioned for any of the men. The citing of diversity as a reason for promotion showed that the diversity initiative was having an impact in the corporation.

Another reflection of corporate personnel objectives has to do with the desire to retain talented candidates who simply were available. One of the reasons given for promotion was that there were people who through no fault of their own were available at a time a particular vacancy occurred. Some of these people were left over from divisions that had been sold. Others were returning from foreign assignments, and still others were managers whose roles were phased out of joint venture projects. These managers were talented, and the corporation wanted to retain them. Availability was mentioned more often for men (38% of the cases) than for women (8%).

Essentially, these data on promotions suggest different dynamics for women and men. Managers seem to be more hesitant to promote women, requiring them to demonstrate personal strength and to prove themselves extensively before they get a promotion. Men were less likely to have their promotion accounted for in terms of familiarity with job responsibilities and were more likely to have bosses report a high level of personal comfort. Managers at this company saw asking women to prove themselves first as a means of providing a safety net for the promotion. The company saw this strategy as a way to give women entry into higher level positions with reduced risk. Unfortunately, the women didn't always experience this as helpful. Although their work was enjoyable, they would have preferred to have had access to key jobs more readily. They felt they weren't getting the same chance to fail or to succeed on their own as the men.

Although the diversity initiative itself was often mentioned as a reason for promotion and bosses were attuned to other corporate personnel objectives such as availability, hiring managers still were not adept at using promotions as a means of giving women challenge and recognition. Bosses tended to have a difficult time determining how much risk to take when making assignment decisions for women subordinates, and it appears that the risk was perceived as greater with women because bosses were less comfortable with these candidates.

In the next section we explore the explanations and implications of these findings. Although the dynamics of promotion we uncovered are thoroughly discussed, there are several caveats to our findings. The first concerns the generalizability of these findings to other organizations. This study was conducted at only one organization and used a small sample. Although our consultation work suggests that the dynamics discussed are experienced more broadly, additional research should be conducted in different settings. A second concern involves the use of retrospective interviews, which are subject to various memory-related biases. Although we interviewed multiple informants about each promotion, the retrospective nature of the study still remains an issue. Further research should explore additional methodologies for studying promotion.

Discussion

In explaining these differences in promotion dynamics between men and women, it is important to consider the various forces at work. The individuals who promote others into key assignments are imperfect evaluators, trying to judge candidates in complex managerial situations. In the company studied, the decision-makers' choices were made in the context of a culture that was changing to become more favorable toward diversity. However, the shift was not yet complete, and some existing organizational structures and policies discouraged diversity. It is the interplay among these forces that created the dynamics seen here.

Decision-making Processes
Promotions to mid- and upper-level management positions require decision-makers to assess individuals in uncertain and complex environments. Such judgments are inherently subjective because of the difficulty of determining the performance of a single individual in the context of interdependent

jobs, complex relationships, ambiguous problem situations, and extended time frames (Dachler, 1989; Ferris & King, 1991; Herriot, 1989; Ruderman & Ohlott, 1994). In response to the lack of clarity with regard to objective performance, decision-makers tend to rely on other sorts of information as proxies in selection decisions (Ferris & King, 1991; Ruderman & Ohlott, 1990). Often these proxies, or signals, are based on personal or social characteristics (Auster, 1989; Kanter, 1977). These signals include, but are not limited to, social similarity, candidate networks, sponsorship of mentors, candidate vulnerability, and candidate visibility.

Perhaps the best known proxy for candidate competence in selection decisions is the reliance on social similarity when performance evaluations are difficult to make (Kanter, 1977). Numerous studies have found that managers tend to prefer working with members of their own sex (Larwood & Blackmore, 1978; Mai-Dalton & Sullivan, 1981; Tsui & O'Reilly, 1989). As social psychologists have pointed out, similarity between individuals is a key component of attraction (Byrne, 1971). In the context of staffing decisions, attraction to the candidate increases the decision-maker's confidence in the candidate (Larwood & Blackmore, 1978). Thus in the face of ambiguous criteria, decision-makers rely on perceived similarity as a way of developing a feeling of comfort with or confidence in the candidate. In terms of our study, this explains why the term *comfort level* was mentioned more often for men than women. The decision-makers, usually males, identified more closely with male candidates and felt more comfortable working with them.

Informal organizational processes, such as networking and mentoring, also contribute to differential promotion dynamics. Ibarra (1993) argues that networks play a role in creating and reinforcing race and gender inequalities in organizations. Network members can provide information about job opportunities to candidates seeking promotion. Ibarra's work suggests decision-makers look at the networks of potential candidates and use this information as a proxy for performance information in evaluation decisions; membership in a high-status network sends the signal to decision-makers that the candidate is powerful, influential, and competent (Brass, 1985; Ibarra, 1993). Because of a well-known tendency to interact with similar others (Kanter, 1977; Tajfel & Turner, 1985), women are often deficient in their contacts with high-status people because they're inclined to network with other women who tend to be outside the power elite of the organization. Thus, women candidates have networks which appear less valuable to the hiring boss.

Another way for a decision-maker to reduce the ambiguity inherent in selection decisions is to give consideration to recommendations from trusted colleagues. Several studies (Kanter, 1977; Ruderman & Ohlott, 1994) found that decision-makers take recommendations about promotion candidates from key organizational players seriously. The advocacy of a candidate by a senior manager acts as a sign to others that she is competent (Kanter, 1977; Kram, 1988). However, evidence suggests the relationships which generate such strong endorsements are less available to women than men because mentoring relationships between senior men and junior women are more complicated than relationships between senior and junior men (Kram, 1988). Because of concerns about intimacy and sexual harassment, cross-gender relationships tend to be more superficial than the men-mentoring-men relationships. Thus, differences in the nature of the relationship make men more likely to have access to someone who can confidently recommend them in a promotion situation than women.

These informal organizational social processes may explain why availability was mentioned more often in promotions of men than women. When men were available, sometimes someone more senior in the organization acted as an advocate. In other cases, information about these men was available through the hiring boss's network. One reason why availability wasn't mentioned often for women may be that when they are available, because of restricted relationships, they may have less knowledge of other opportunities and fewer alliances to help them find key positions.

Another force that contributes to differential dynamics in promotion is what Kram and McCollom (in press) have called the visibility-vulnerability spiral. Women in leadership positions in organizations experience heightened visibility because of their minority status. This visibility makes them more watched and hence more vulnerable to criticism and attack. This vulnerability (whether perceived or actual) adds a cost to promoting a woman. In the ambiguous context of promotion decisions, vulnerability can be interpreted by a decision-maker as evidence of a lack of competence. Vulnerability can be an asset because it can lead to learning about self, others, and the system one is attempting to lead. However, women are still perceived as the weaker sex, and weakness in a leader makes followers fear for the success and survival of their group when faced with competition from other groups. Decision-makers may also think that putting a vulnerable leader in charge of a group makes the whole group vulnerable. The visibility-vulnerability spiral means that decision-makers are likely to see promoting women as riskier than promoting men, because they feel they are putting a woman in jeopardy by putting her in a leadership role. We suspect that the heightened vulnerability women experience is the reason why personal strength was mentioned for only the women in the study and not the men.

Although the vulnerability women experience may bring an added cost to hiring them, the associated visibility may be a benefit. The promotion of a woman is likely to result in increased visibility for the decision-maker as well. In the organization studied, promoting a woman was seen as an example of compliance with the diversity initiative. This is important because the CEO is publicly and privately committed to diversity, and promoting women demonstrates support of the CEO's stance. The rational bias theory of discrimination (Larwood, Szwajkowski, & Rose, 1988) suggests managers making promotion decisions consider the effects the decisions might have on their own careers. Managers making promotion decisions are more likely to promote women if individuals who hold power over these managers stress it is important to do so.

The Formal Push Toward Diversity

The combination of this push from the organization toward greater diversity and the problems inherent in evaluating promotion candidates created some subtle, yet powerful, dynamics in this organization: pacification by promotion and intense scrutiny in the evaluation process.

Flanders and Anderson (1973) first identified the practice of pacifying women by promotion, referring to the finding that it takes women more promotions than men to reach a particular pay level. In the context of the company studied, we suggest that management created the appearance of improved opportunity, responsibility, and recognition for women; when in reality, the situation changed only slightly. In other words, some of the promotions investigated appeared to have happened in two steps. Women first move to new positions with increased responsibilities and then later, after proving themselves, receive the commensurate pay and title, rendering the second promotion hollow to many of the women. Decision-makers thought they could pacify both the women and senior management by promoting women in small increments.

In addition, the frequency with which continuity was mentioned for the women suggests that women were more closely scrutinized over a period of time. In several cases, women got promoted into situations where they already had been watched closely and had demonstrated competence, suggesting that the male decision-makers were uncomfortable taking risks in giving assignments to women (O'Leary & Ickovics, 1992). In contrast, the promotions of men tended to involve a greater increase in the scope of new responsibilities, with less opportunity to observe them handling the new responsibilities prior to the promotion. We suspect that this scrutiny acted as a means of making the decision-makers more comfortable with the women candidates by giving decision-makers time to work through some of their biases. This style of promotion results in a reluctance to give women challenging assignments, which are vital to the success of the group.

Consequences for Individual Development

This cautious style of promoting women has critical implications. Taking fewer risks with the promotions of women limits the degree of reward and challenge experienced by individual women managers. Morrison (1992) has identified these factors—reward and challenge—as two of the three key forces in management development. Both the experience of hollow promotions and the intense scrutiny that precedes promotions lessen the impact of these
factors.

One of the key outcomes of a promotion is the reward value for the individual (Markham, Harlan, & Hackett, 1987). Promotions bring with them the recognition that the individual is seen as a person of potential. The reward associated with a promotion is lessened, however, if the promotion was given after greater responsibility had already been assumed. The extreme caution demonstrated by the decision-makers lessens the power of the promotion as a reward.

Another characteristic of promotions is that they offer the job challenge necessary for development (McCall et al., 1988). Challenging jobs are the backbone of management development, with the degree of transition between two jobs being a major component of development (Morrow, Ruderman, & McCauley, 1992). Transitions, such as promotions, are particularly developmental because they confront managers with novel situations rendering existing routines and behaviors inadequate and they require the development of new skills to cope with the problems and opportunities (Nicholson & West, 1988). Unfortunately, the greater cautiousness taken in the promotion of women can limit the challenge needed for further development. If promotions for women tend to be for positions similar to what they have done before, there is less of a transition and hence less opportunity for development.

A further complication of taking extra caution with women is that, according to Auster (1989), it creates a catch-22 with regard to further career advancement. The lower the value of the task a woman receives, the greater the justification for not considering her for further promotions. Cautiousness about one job move on the part of a decision-maker actually hurts the candidate's chances for further development and advancement.

Further implications of the study have to do with the mention of diversity goals as a reason for promotion. One implication may be that the organization is taking the initiative to heart, and the climate for diversity is changing in the desired direction. Other evidence that the diversity initiative is doing well can be drawn from the fact that we found more similarities than differences in the promotions of men and women; it is especially promising that qualifications, performance, and experience were the most important factors in promotions for both men and women.

The problem, though, with diversity coming up as a reason for promotion is the impact of this promotion rationale on the women themselves. Attribution theory suggests that men's successful performance is attributed to internal factors, such as ability, and women's successful performance tends to be attributed to external factors (Cash, Gillen, & Burns, 1977; Deaux & Emswiller, 1974). Thus, the publicity around the diversity initiative itself may make women doubt their competence by causing them to question if they were promoted because of diversity pressures rather than their qualifications. It may also affect how they are viewed by others and contribute to the extra scrutiny women managers receive. This becomes particularly problematic in light of our findings that with regard to most of the reasons for promotion, there were no differences in the promotions of men and women.

Although our study has focused on promotion dynamics for women, we suspect that the dynamics would be similar for people of color. Issues around comfort level, social similarity, networks, visibility-vulnerability, and reluctance to take risks would be just as applicable to any members of nondominant groups in organizations.

Implications: Enhancing the Promotion Decision Process

This study suggests that the promotion decision process may unintentionally undermine corporate objectives to improve managerial diversity. Even with clear intentions to develop and promote women (and people of color), several subtle yet potent dynamics can perpetuate systematically differential treatment of dominant and nondominant groups. In particular, the findings suggest that male decision-makers tend to choose men for promotions because of a perceived comfort level, and they choose women for the personal strength they exhibit or the familiarity (tenure) and continuity they already have in a particular job situation. In an effort to make the best decision for the company (and for the individual), women may be kept longer in assignments in order to insure readiness and to minimize risk. Left unexamined, these dynamics perpetuate slower movement of women into leadership positions.

Our view is that these promotion decision dynamics must be made visible and discussible so that decision-makers can better understand their unintended consequences and, in turn, practices can be modified to truly support managerial diversity. Consultations with several organizations suggest several strategies for accomplishing these ends, including: (1) assessing current practices, (2) modifying human resources systems and practices to improve accountability, and (3) providing opportunities for personal learning.

Assessment of Current Practices

Several types and sources of information on current practices enable decision-makers to achieve an accurate understanding of promotion decisions. First, it is useful to obtain objective data regarding both retention and promotion. These serve to clarify whether barriers to leadership diversity exist in early socialization practices, early development practices, and in management- and executive-development practices. Second, it is equally important to obtain subjective data regarding perceptions of promotions practices, both from decision-makers and promotion candidates.

Asking the human resources function to track retention rates, promotion rates, and patterns of job movement for members of dominant and non-dominant groups can help identify practices that are undermining leadership diversity. For example, if turnover is higher among women and people of color, particularly in the first five years of employment, attention can then be given to early socialization and mentoring processes to insure that non-traditionals are given adequate support, guidance, and recognition (Morrison, 1992). Higher turnover rates also suggest the possibility that (in an effort to achieve more diversity through hiring) candidates from diverse backgrounds are given unrealistic expectations during the recruiting process, leading to disappointment and frustration as reality sets in.

In contrast, if retention rates at junior levels are similar, but promotion to middle and senior levels are substantially lower for women and people of color, then attention must be given to development practices for experienced high performers. For example, if it takes women more moves to reach a particular level than men, then the company is probably promoting men and women in different ways. Women, in this scenario, would likely be moved in two steps rather than one. This explains why continuity and pushing for the job were often given as reasons for promoting women in the company studied here.

Decision-makers frequently are perplexed by the latter discrepancy. Through interviews that prompt reflection on one's assumptions, perceptions, and strategies for developing diversity in leadership, and through examination of data from interviews with promotion candidates (from both dominant and nondominant groups), the assumptions, stereotypes, and intergroup processes that shape promotion decisions and development practices can be made visible. In trying to make sense of these data, some executives begin to understand their role in creating the subtle yet potent dynamics outlined earlier.

Modifications in Human Resources Systems and Practices

Organizations that are most successful in achieving managerial diversity clearly have human resources systems and practices that hold managers and executives accountable for achieving diversity objectives and encourage them to actively develop women and people of color (Cox, 1993). Indeed this infrastructure directly shapes promotion decisions by influencing decision-makers' priorities and actions. Succession planning, performance appraisal and reward systems, and development practices can either perpetuate those dynamics that undermine adequate promotion of women or help to create dynamics that insure successful advancement.

Meaningful accountability is established through a clearly articulated vision and mechanisms for holding individuals responsible for achieving managerial diversity in their business units. This means that business plans and succession plans will have diversity objectives at their core, and that leaders will regularly review (in the formal appraisal process) whether individuals are taking sufficient actions to recruit, develop, and ultimately promote women to leadership roles. Those who achieve diversity objectives will be adequately recognized through compensation and other rewards. Accountability alone is not sufficient, however. Organizations emphasizing diversity goals must be careful to avoid the pitfalls around attributions discussed earlier, lest women begin to doubt their own competence.

The existence of diversity objectives doesn't insure sincere attention to their accomplishment. Indeed, in several organizations that we have worked with, senior executives who were most concerned about achieving diversity noted that some of their peers and subordinates didn't really believe that performance and rewards were influenced by their efforts to develop and promote women and people of color. In these same organizations managers at all levels commented that when it comes to recognition and rewards, business results—not diversity results—are what matter. Similarly, in the study reported here, the subtle rationales bosses gave for their promotion decisions reflect the organizational cultures and values of what is rewarded. If managers who fail to achieve diversity objectives are not penalized, then the impact of a system of accountability is diminished.

Perceptions of what the organization rewards inevitably erode attention to the challenges posed by an increasingly diverse workforce. Not only do business pressures generally drive out attention to development, but executives under pressure fall back on doing what they know best—developing individuals like themselves. Too often, when asked why they have been unable to identify, develop, and promote high-performing nontraditionals, the response is that there are insufficient women and people of color in the pipeline.

Upon further scrutiny it often becomes evident that failure to achieve diversity objectives has more to do with the discomfort white male executives experience as they attempt to mentor and coach people of different backgrounds, or the reluctance and risk they feel at the prospect of giving people who are different the most challenging assignments (Kram & Bragar, 1992; Kram & Hall, in press). Individuals of varied backgrounds have been recruited and retained in the first five years, but attention to their development after the initial entry period has been insufficient.

Closing the gap between intentions to achieve diversity and actual practice can best be done by creating accountability to the group, rather than only to one's superior. Well-managed organizations have found that decisions about key assignments are best deliberated in a group context in order to benefit from multiple perspectives on particular candidates and to insure that biases outlined earlier don't govern critical decisions (Hall, 1986; Hall & Foulkes, 1991). In settings where there is an increasingly diverse pool of candidates to draw upon, there is mounting evidence—including the study reported here—that without this careful group deliberation, executives will tend to choose candidates with whom they feel most comfortable and who are most similar to them (Hall, 1994).

Two other mechanisms exist for strengthening accountability for developing and promoting nontraditionals. First, formal mentoring programs that match senior executives with high-potential managers insure that nontraditionals are given the support, recognition, and challenge that are so critical for further advancement (Kram & Bragar, 1992; Kram & Hall, in press; Murray & Owen, 1991). Such formalized programs insure that individuals, who otherwise might find it difficult to obtain adequate coaching and exposure, have access to this essential developmental process. These initiatives strengthen accountability when the actions taken by designated mentors to coach and develop their assigned protégés are regularly reviewed and incorporated into appraisal and compensation decisions.

Second, when formal matching programs don't fit with a more organic and fluid culture, executives can develop action plans in which they identify: (1) specific nontraditionals who they will actively develop through ongoing coaching and developmental assignments and (2) other actions they can take to insure a supportive and growth-inducing environment for people of diverse backgrounds (for example, holding their subordinates accountable for coaching and mentoring, insuring assignments are fairly distributed, and creating opportunities to discuss the challenges posed by diversity).

Provision of Personal Opportunities for Learning

An infrastructure of human resources systems and practices that encourages attention to diversity issues is essential but certainly not sufficient to insure that promotion decisions enable high-performing women to successfully advance to senior positions. Equally important are opportunities for decision-makers to deepen their awareness of their role in perpetuating the dynamics outlined earlier, to develop the competencies to mentor women and people of color, and to learn new approaches to development that truly support managerial diversity. Without work of this kind, it is all too likely that diversity objectives will not be achieved. Several alternatives exist for promoting such personal learning.

First, education and training that enable individuals to learn the coaching and counseling skills so fundamental to the mentoring process are now widely available. (For resources on such education and training designs see, for example: Kram, 1988; Phillips-Jones, 1993; Shea, 1992.) Most of these seminars or workshops provide the opportunity for individuals to practice the fundamental skills of listening, feedback, and coaching, as well as to develop the self-awareness and interpersonal skills to build relationships that cross gender, racial, and cultural boundaries. The underlying assumption is that with mastery of these requisite skills, executives will be more willing and able to develop and promote individuals of diverse backgrounds.

An important limitation of this alternative, however, is that many executives are unwilling to attend such off-site educational events because of business pressures. In addition, one-time educational experiences may not be as impactful and enduring as learning that occurs on the job. Recently, several researchers and practitioners delineated core competencies—including listening, reflecting on one's own knowledge and experience, articulating one's assumptions, and the willingness to suspend one's personal beliefs in order to learn from another's point of view—that are now considered essential to individual success and organizational survival (see, for example: Isaacs, 1993; Schon, 1990; Senge, 1990). These are best mastered through a process called *dialogue*—conversations with colleagues that enable substantial personal learning to occur in the context of relationships with individuals of different backgrounds (Walker & Hansen, 1992).

In some instances, however, the prospect of setting up such a learning group is perceived as impractical, burdensome, and threatening. Then, other vehicles for promoting dialogue must be invented. In an organization one author has worked with, executives who began to learn from the assessment of current practices agreed to have one conversation with a woman in their business unit to inquire about perceived barriers to their own advancement. These executives were given guidelines and suggested questions that structured an effective dialogue process. One week later they exuded enthusiasm in a meeting where they reported all that they had learned in one conversation. This was the beginning of an ongoing dialogue with junior women that would enable relationship-building and learning about diversity issues to continue.

A final alternative for fostering personal learning among decision-makers is executive coaching. (For discussion of the benefits and limitations of coaching in its various forms, see for example: Kinlaw, 1993; Mink, Owen, & Mink, 1993; Pryor, 1994; Smith, 1993.) Both internal and external coaches are increasingly viewed as key resources in helping individuals learn from their own experience, particularly when time is very limited and developing new competencies and perspectives is essential. In combination with 360-degree feedback, regular appraisals, and other vehicles outlined here, a coaching relationship can provide a safe environment in which decision-makers explore how their own assumptions, values, and behaviors perpetuate promotion decisions that undermine managerial diversity. Through such personal inquiry, executives develop new ways to approach development and promotion issues.

Conclusion

This study highlights how the promotion decision process can undermine women's advancement, even in organizations (like the one studied here) that are known for their progressive work on a number of diversity-related concerns. Without careful examination of the subtle yet potent dynamics that shape assignments and promotion decisions, it is likely that decision-makers will continue to choose candidates with whom they feel most comfortable and will utilize systematically different criteria for promoting men and women.

Through collaborations with several firms committed to reducing barriers to nontraditionals' advancement to senior management, we have clarified several strategies for making these complex dynamics visible and discussible. Although the particular combination of strategies will vary depending on the vision, culture, and practices of the firm, a combination of assessing current practices, an infrastructure of accountability for proactive development of women and people of color, and opportunities for personal inquiry will enable decision-makers to make promotions an effective diversity practice. Then, actual results will come into better alignment with espoused diversity objectives and intent.

References

Auster, E. (1989). Task characteristics as a bridge between macro- and micro-level research on salary inequality between men and women. *Academy of Management Review, 14*, 173-193.

Brass, D. J. (1985). Men's and women's networks: A study of interaction patterns and influence in an organization. *Academy of Management Journal, 28*, 327-343.

Byrne, D. (1971). *The attraction paradigm.* New York: Academic Press.

Cash, T. F., Gillen, B., & Burns, D. S. (1977). Sexism and "beautyism" in personnel consultant decision making. *Journal of Applied Psychology, 62*, 301-310.

Catalyst. (1990). *Women in corporate management: Results of a Catalyst survey.* New York: Catalyst.

Cox, T. (1993). *Cultural diversity in organizations.* San Francisco: Berrett-Koehler.

Dachler, H. P. (1989). Selection and the organizational culture. In P. Herriot (Ed.), *Handbook of assessment in organizations* (pp. 45-80). New York: John Wiley.

Deaux, K., & Emswiller, T. (1974). Explanations of successful performance in sex-linked tasks: What is skill for the male is luck for the female. *Journal of Personality and Social Psychology, 29*, 80-85.

Ferris, G. R., Buckley, M. R., & Allen, G. M. (1992). Promotion systems in organizations. *Human Resource Planning, 15*(3), 47-68.

Ferris, G. R., & King, T. R. (1991). Politics in human resource decisions: A walk on the dark side. *Organizational Dynamics, 20*(2), 59-71.

Flanders, D. P., & Anderson, P. E. (1973). Sex discrimination in employment: Theory and practice. *Industrial and Labor Relations Review, 26*, 938-955.

Hall, D. T. (1986). Dilemmas in linking succession planning to individual executive learning. *Human Resource Management, 25*(1), 235-265.

Hall, D. T. (1994). *Executive careers and learning: Aligning selection and development.* Technical Report, Executive Development Roundtable, Boston University School of Management.

Hall, D. T., & Foulkes, F. K. (1991). Senior executive development as a competitive advantage. *Advances in Applied Business Strategy, 2*, 183-203.

Hays, W. L. (1973). *Statistics for the social sciences.* New York: Holt, Rinehart and Winston.

Herriot, P. (1989). Selection as a social process. In M. Smith & I. T. Robertson (Eds.), *Advances in selection and assessment* (pp. 171-187). New York: John Wiley.

Ibarra, H. (1993). Personal networks of women and minorities in management: A conceptual framework. *Academy of Management Review, 18*, 56-87.

Isaacs, W. N. (1993, Autumn). Taking flight: Dialogue, collective thinking, and organizational learning. *Organizational Dynamics,* pp. 24-39.

Kanter, R. M. (1977). *Men and women of the corporation.* New York: Basic Books.

Kinlaw, D. C. (1993). *Coaching for commitment*. San Diego: Pfeiffer.

Kram, K. E. (1988). *Mentoring at work: Developmental relationships in organizational life*. Lanham, MD: University Press of America.

Kram, K. E., & Bragar, M. E. (1992). Development through mentoring: A strategic approach. In D. Montross & C. Shinkman (Eds.), *Career development: Theory and practice* (pp. 221-254). Chicago: Charles C. Thomas.

Kram, K. E., & Hall, D. T. (in press). Mentoring in a context of diversity and turbulence. In E. E. Kossek & S. Lobel (Eds.), *Human resource strategies for managing diversity*. London: Blackwell Publishers.

Kram, K. E., & McCollom, M. E. (in press). When women lead: The visibility-vulnerability spiral. In E. B. Klein & F. Gabelnick (Eds.), *New paradigms for leadership in the twenty-first century*. New York: John Wiley.

Larwood, L., & Blackmore, J. (1978). Sex discrimination in managerial selection: Testing predictions of the vertical dyad linkage model. *Sex Roles, 4,* 359-367.

Larwood, L., Szwajkowski, P., & Rose, S. (1988). When discrimination makes "sense"—The rational bias theory of discrimination. In B. A. Gutek, A. H. Stromberg, & L. Larwood (Eds.), *Women and work* (pp. 265-288). Newbury Park, CA: Sage.

Mai-Dalton, R. R., & Sullivan, J. J. (1981). The effects of manager's sex on the assignment to a challenging or dull task and reasons for the choice. *Academy of Management Journal, 24,* 603-612.

Markham, W. T., Harlan, S. L., & Hackett, E. J. (1987). Promotion opportunities in organization: Causes and consequences. In K. M. Rowland & G. R. Ferris (Eds.), *Research in personnel and human resources management* (Vol. 5). Greenwich, CT: JAI Press.

McCall, M. W., Jr., Lombardo, M. M., & Morrison, A. M. (1988). *The lessons of experience: How successful executives develop on the job*. Lexington, MA: Lexington Books.

Mink, O. G., Owen, K. Q., & Mink, B. P. (1993). *Developing high performance people: The art of coaching*. Reading, MA: Addison-Wesley.

Morrison, A. M. (1992). *The new leaders: Guidelines for leadership diversity in America*. San Francisco: Jossey-Bass.

Morrow, J. E., Ruderman, M. N., & McCauley, C. D. (1992). *On-the-job learning and transitions to new organizational levels*. In the symposium: Understanding Managerial Transitions, chaired by M. N. Ruderman. Society for Industrial and Organizational Psychology, Inc.

Murray, M., & Owen, M. A. (1991). *Beyond the myths and magic of mentoring: How to facilitate an effective mentoring program*. San Francisco: Jossey-Bass.

Nicholson, N., & West, M. (1988). *Managerial job change: Men and women in transition*. Cambridge, England: Cambridge University Press.

O'Leary, V. E., & Ickovics, J. R. (1992). Cracking the glass ceiling: Overcoming isolation and alienation. In U. Sekaran & F. T. Leong (Eds.), *Womanpower: Managing in times of demographic turbulence* (pp. 7-30). New York: Sage.

Perry, E. L., Davis-Blake, A., & Kulik, C. (1994). Explaining gender-based selection decision: A synthesis of contextual and cognitive approaches. *Academy of Management Review, 19,* 786-820.

Phillips-Jones, L. L. (1993). *The mentoring program design package* (2nd ed.). Grass Valley, CA: Coalition of Counseling Centers.

Powell, G. N., & Maniero, L. A. (1992). Cross-currents in the river of time: Conceptualizing the complexities of women's careers. *Journal of Management, 18*(2), 215-237.

Pryor, S. E. (1994). *Executive coaching: Sign of stigma or success?* Technical Report, Executive Development Roundtable, School of Management, Boston University.

Rosen, B., & Jerdee, T. H. (1974). Effect of applicant sex and difficulty of job on evaluations of candidates for managerial positions. *Journal of Applied Psychology, 59,* 511-512.

Rosenbaum, J. E. (1979). Tournament mobility: Career patterns in a corporation. *Administrative Science Quarterly, 24,* 220-241.

Ruderman, M. N., & Ohlott, P. J. (1990). *Traps and pitfalls in the judgment of executive potential* (Report No. 141). Greensboro, NC: Center for Creative Leadership.

Ruderman, M. N., & Ohlott, P. J. (1994). *The realities of management promotion* (Report No. 157). Greensboro, NC: Center for Creative Leadership.

Schon, D. A. (1990). *Educating the reflective practitioner.* San Francisco: Jossey-Bass.

Senge, P. M. (1990). *The fifth discipline: The art and practice of the learning organization.* New York: Doubleday.

Sharpe, R. (1994, March 29). The waiting game: Women make strides, but men stay firmly in top company jobs. *The Wall Street Journal,* pp. A1, A10.

Shea, G. F. (1992). *Mentoring: How to develop successful mentor behaviors.* Los Altos, CA: Crips Publications.

Smith, L. (1993, December). The executive's new coach. *Fortune,* pp. 126-134.

Tajfel, H., & Turner, J. (1985). The social identity theory of intergroup behavior. In S. Worchel & W. Austing (Eds.), *Psychology of intergroup behavior* (pp. 7-24). Chicago: Nelson-Hall.

Thomas, P. J. (1989). Appraising the performance of women: Gender and the naval officer. In B. A. Gutek & L. Larwood (Eds.), *Women's career development* (pp. 86-109). New York: Sage.

Tsui, A. S., & O'Reilly, C. (1989). Beyond simple demographic effects: Relational demography in superior-subordinate dyads. *Academy of Management Journal, 32,* 402-423.

Walker, B. A., & Hanson, W. C. (1992). Valuing differences at Digital Equipment Corporation. In S. Jackson & Associates (Eds.), *Diversity in the workplace: Human resource initiatives* (pp. 119-137). New York: Guilford Press.

Appendix

Primary Interview Questions

We asked decision-makers (the boss and the boss's boss) the following questions about the person promoted and the promotion decision:

(1) Tell me about how you decided to place _____ in this position. When did the vacancy arise? How did the vacancy arise?

(2) What are the major responsibilities facing _____?

(3) For how long have you known _____? When did you first meet? How did you first hear of _____?

(4) If you were restricted to only one reason why you selected _____ for this position, what would it be? What would a second reason be? Other reasons?

(5) What was it that brought _____ to your attention for this position?

(6) Were there other candidates for the position? Why weren't they selected?

(7) How did you get information about the candidates?

(8) Was this promotion a success?

We asked similar questions of the people promoted:

(1) What is your current job? What are its duties and responsibilities?

(2) What people do you think had a part in your promotion decision? How long have you known each of them? What is your relationship to each of them?

(3)   If you were allowed to describe only one reason why you think you were selected for this position, what would it be? How did you know that? When do you think people first realized that about you?

(4)   What would a second reason be? Any other reasons?

(5)   Who else was considered for your job? Why do you think they were not selected?

Human resources managers familiar with the cases were asked:

(1)   What is _____'s background? What are _____'s major responsibilities in this job?

(2)   How did the vacancy occur?

(3)   Who was involved in the promotion decision?

(4)   Was anyone else considered for the position? Why weren't they selected?

(5)   What was the single most important reason _____ was promoted?

(6)   What were other reasons?

Ordering Information

To get more information, to order additional **CCL Press** publications, or to find out about bulk-order discounts, please contact us by phone at **336-545-2810** or visit our online bookstore at **www. ccl.org/publications**.